Hip 2 B square

BABY wraps

Introducing Melissa Leapman's fresh mix-and-match squares—the hip way to get creative with crochet!

Hip 2 B Square Baby Wraps lets you choose from 15 fun motifs. Make the squares you like—then whipstitch them into a blanket any baby will love. Can't decide which squares you like best? Let one of the five inspiration projects get you going!

Turn to page 31 to discover how you can add more *Hip 2 B Square* motifs and projects to your crochet pattern library!

"It was great fun designing the *Hip 2 B Square* leaflet series." Melissa Leapman says. "I love the way all the squares work together in a mix-and-match fashion. A crocheter can choose one or two motifs to create a project, or combine several different ones.

"I hope these interchangeable squares will bring many hours of stitching fun to crocheters of all skill levels, all over the country!"

LEISURE ARTS, INC.
Little Rock, Arkansas

Finished Size: 38" x 50"
(96.5 cm x 127 cm)

MATERIALS

Light Weight Yarn
[5 ounces, 395 yards
(140 grams, 361 meters)
per skein]:
 Lilac - 7 skeins
Crochet hook, size G (4 mm)
 or size needed for gauge
Yarn needle

GAUGE: Each Square = 6"
(15 cm)

SQUARES

Make 48 Ribbed Squares,
page 18, using Lilac for
Color D.

Block each Square to measure
6" (15 cm) **(see Blocking,
page 29)**.

ASSEMBLY

With **wrong** sides together
and using photo as a guide
for placement, whipstitch
Squares together **(Figs. 5a & b,
page 29)**, alternating direction
of Squares and forming
6 vertical strips of 8 Squares
each, beginning and ending in
corners; then whipstitch strips
together in same manner.

EDGING

Rnd 1: With **right** side facing,
join yarn with sc in any corner
st **(see Joining With Sc,
page 27)**; work an odd number
of sc along each side working
one sc in each corner; join with
slip st to first sc.

Rnd 2: Ch 4 **(counts as first
dc plus ch 1)**, do **not** turn; (dc,
ch 1) twice in same st, ★ skip
next sc, (dc in next sc, ch 1, skip
next sc) across to next corner
sc, (dc, ch 1) 3 times in corner
sc; repeat from ★ 2 times **more**,
skip next sc, (dc in next sc, ch 1,
skip next sc) across; join with
slip st to first dc.

To work Picot, ch 3, slip st in
third ch from hook.

Rnd 3: Ch 1, (sc, work Picot,
sc) in next ch-1 sp and in each
ch-1 sp around; join with slip st
to first sc, finish off.

alternating RIB WRAP

HIP 2 B square

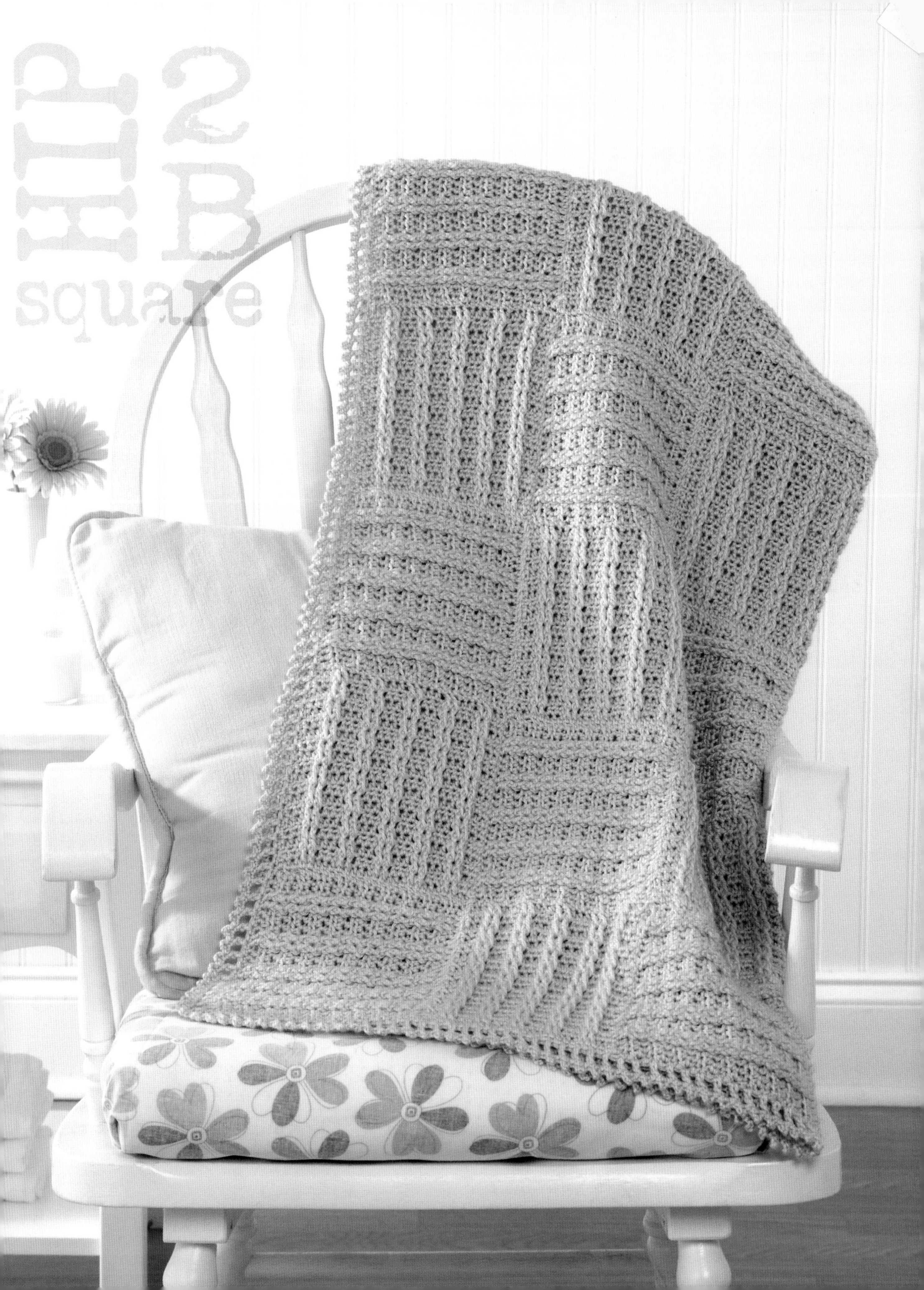

Finished Size: 37" x 49"
(94 cm x 124.5 cm)

MATERIALS

Light Weight Yarn
[5 ounces, 459 yards
(141 grams, 420 meters
per skein]:
    Violet - 2 skeins
    Yellow - 1 skein
    Purple - 1 skein
    White - 1 skein
    Mint - 1 skein
Crochet hook, size G (4 mm)
   or size needed for gauge
Yarn needle

Note: The colors used for this wrap are the ones used in the Stitch Gallery Color Key, page 12.

GAUGE: Each Square = 6"
(15 cm)

SQUARES

Make a total of 48 Squares.
Make 3 **each**:
1. Basketweave, page 14.
2. Checkerboard, page 14.
3. Chrysanthemum, page 15.
4. Circles in the Square, page 16.
7. Eyelet, page 18.
8. Daisy, page 19.
10. Lacy V-Stitch, page 21.
13. Multicolored, page 23.
14. Star, page 24.
15. Teardrops, page 25.

Make 2 **each**:
5. Concentric Circles, page 17.
6. Ribbed, page 18.
12. Crossed Stitch Stripes, page 22.

Make 8:
9. Diagonal Stripes, page 20.

Make 4:
11. Griddle Stitch, page 21.

Block each Square to measure 6" (15 cm) **(see Blocking, page 29)**.

ASSEMBLY

With **wrong** sides together and using Placement Diagram as a guide, whipstitch Squares together **(Figs. 5a & b, page 29)**, forming 6 vertical strips of 8 Squares each, beginning and ending in corners; then whipstitch strips together in same manner.

EDGING

With **right** side facing, join White with dc in any st; dc evenly around working 3 dc in each corner; join with slip st to first dc, finish off.

* Turn Diagonal Stripes Squares to match arrow directions.

Placement Diagram

1	3	2	11	13	4
14	7	8	10	5	15
4	9* ↗↙	12	13	9* ↘↖	6
3	11	9* ↗↙	9* ↘↖	15	10
7	2	9* ↘↖	9* ↙↗	1	8
4	9* ↘↖	14	12	9* ↗↙	11
15	5	10	8	7	14
6	13	11	2	3	1

Finished Size: 38" x 50"
(96.5 cm x 127 cm)

MATERIALS
Light Weight Yarn
[7 ounces, 575 yards
(198 grams, 525 meters)
per skein]:
   White - 2 skeins
   Blue, Green, Mint, Pink,
   Yellow - 1 skein **each**
Crochet hook, size G (4 mm)
  or size needed for gauge
Yarn needle

GAUGE: Each Square = 6"
(15 cm)

SQUARES
Make a total of 48 Concentric
Circles Squares, page 17,
making 8 **each** using Blue,
Green, Mint, Pink and Yellow for
Color E.

Block each Square to measure
6" (15 cm) **(see Blocking,
page 29)**.

ASSEMBLY
With **wrong** sides together,
whipstitch Squares together
randomly as desired **(Figs.
5a & b, page 29)**, forming 6
vertical strips of 8 Squares
each, beginning and ending in
corners; then whipstitch strips
together in same manner.

EDGING
With **right** side facing, join White
with dc in any st; dc evenly
around working 3 dc in each
corner; join with slip st to first dc
finish off.

concentric CIRCLES WRAP

Finished Size: 37" x 49"
(94 cm x 124.5 cm)

MATERIALS
Light Weight Yarn
[3 ounces, 279 yards
(85 grams, 255 meters)
per skein]:
    Blue - 5 skeins
    White - 2 skeins
    Green - 3 skeins
Crochet hook, size G (4 mm)
   or size needed for gauge
Yarn needle

GAUGE: Each Square = 6"
(15 cm)

SQUARES
Make 12 Chrysanthemum
Squares, page 15, using Blue
for Color A and White for
Color D.

Make 12 Daisy Squares,
page 19, using Blue for
Color A, Green for Color E and
White for Color D.

Make 12 Basketweave
Squares, page 14, making 6
each using Blue and Green for
Color E.

Make 12 Griddle Stitch
Squares, page 21, making 6
each using Blue and Green for
Color A.

Block each Square to measure
6" (15 cm) **(see Blocking,
page 29)**.

ASSEMBLY
With **wrong** sides together
and using photo as a guide,
whipstitch Squares together
(Figs. 5a & b, page 29),
alternating Squares and
forming 6 vertical strips of
8 Squares each, beginning
and ending in corners; then
whipstitch strips together in
same manner.

EDGING
With **right** side facing, join Blue
with dc in any st; dc evenly
around working 3 dc in each
corner; join with slip st to first
dc, finish off.

FOUR Square WRAP

Finished Size: 38" x 50"
(96.5 cm x 127 cm)

MATERIALS
Light Weight Yarn 3
[5 ounces, 395 yards
(140 grams, 361 meters)
per skein]:
    Yellow - 3 skeins
    Blue - 2 skeins
    Mint - 2 skeins
Crochet hook, size G (4 mm)
or size needed for gauge
Yarn needle

GAUGE: Each Square = 6"
(15 cm)

SQUARE
Make 24 Eyelet Squares,
page 18.

Make 24 Star Squares,
page 24, using Yellow for
Color D, Blue for Color A, and
Mint for Color C.

Block each Square to measure
6" (15 cm) **(see Blocking,
page 29)**.

ASSEMBLY
With **wrong** sides together
and using photo as a guide,
whipstitch Squares together
(Figs. 5a & b, page 29),
alternating Squares and
forming 6 vertical strips of
8 Squares each, beginning
and ending in corners; then
whipstitch strips together in
same manner.

EDGING
Rnd 1: With **right** side facing,
join Mint with sc in any corner
st; work an odd number of sc
along each side working one sc
in each corner; join with slip st
to first sc.

Rnd 2: Ch 4 **(counts as first
dc plus ch 1)**, do **not** turn; (dc,
ch 1) twice in same st, ★ skip
next sc, (dc in next sc, ch 1,
skip next sc) across to next
corner sc, (dc, ch 1) 3 times
in corner sc; repeat from ★
2 times **more**, skip next sc,
(dc in next sc, ch 1, skip next
sc) across; join with slip st to
first dc.

To work Picot, ch 3, slip st in
third ch from hook.

Rnd 3: Ch 1, (sc, work Picot,
sc) in next ch-1 sp and in each
ch-1 sp around; join with slip st
to first sc, finish off.

star & eyelet WRAP

stitch
GALLERY

Instructions for all Squares are on pages 14-25.

Finished Size: 6" (15 cm) square

We used Light Weight Yarn  and a size G (4 mm) crochet hook for all the photographed Squares. **Use the size hook needed to achieve a 6" (15 cm) square.**

Color Key
Color A (Violet)
Color B (Yellow)
Color C (Purple)
Color D (White)
Color E (Mint)

8

9

10

11

12

13

14

15

HIP 2 B

square

basketweave

■■□□□ EASY

Yarn Requirements for one square:
Color E - 63 yards
(57.5 meters)

GAUGE: In pattern,
10 sts = 2" (5 cm)

Ch 30.

Row 1 (Right side): Dc in fourth ch from hook **(3 skipped chs count as first dc)** and in each ch across: 28 dc.

Note: Loop a short piece of yarn around any dc to mark Row 1 as **right** side.

To work Front Post double crochet (abbreviated FPdc), YO, insert hook from **front** to **back** around post of st indicated **(Fig. 2, page 28)**, YO and pull up a loop (3 loops on hook), (YO and draw through 2 loops on hook) twice.

To work Back Post double crochet (abbreviated BPdc), YO, insert hook from **back** to **front** around post of st indicated **(Fig. 2, page 28)**, YO and pull up a loop (3 loops on hook), (YO and draw through 2 loops on hook) twice.

Row 2: Ch 2 **(counts as first hdc)**, turn; work FPdc around each of next 2 sts, (work BPdc around each of next 2 sts, work FPdc around each of next 2 sts) across to last st, hdc in last st.

Repeat Row 2 for pattern until piece measures approximately 6" (15 cm) from beginning ch.

Finish off leaving a long end for sewing.

checkerboard

■■□□□ EASY

Yarn Requirements for one square:
Color B - 25 yards
(23 meters)
Color E - 25 yards
(23 meters)

GAUGE: In pattern,
16 dc = 3" (7.5 cm)

With Color B, ch 32.

Row 1 (Right side): Dc in fourth ch from hook **(3 skipped chs count as first dc)**, dc in next ch changing to Color E **(Figs. 1a-c, page 27)**, dc in next 3 chs changing to Color B, ★ dc in next 3 chs changing to Color E, dc in next 3 chs changing to Color B; repeat from ★ across: 30 dc.

Note: Loop a short piece of yarn around any dc to mark Row 1 as **right** side.

Row 2: Ch 3 **(counts as first dc)**, turn; dc in next 2 dc changing to Color E, dc in next 3 dc changing to Color B, ★ dc in next 3 dc changing to Color E, dc in next 3 dc changing to Color B; repeat from ★ across.

Repeat Row 2 for pattern until Square measures approximately 6" (15 cm) from beginning ch, ending by working a **right** side row.

Finish off leaving a long end for sewing.

chrysanthemum

■■□□ EASY

**Yarn Requirements for
one square:**
Color A - 18 yards
(16.5 meters)
Color D - 27 yards
(24.5 meters)

GAUGE: Rnds 1 and 2 = 2¹/₂"
(6.25 cm) diameter

With Color A, ch 6; join with
slip st to form a ring.

Rnd 1 (Right side)**:** Ch 1, ★ sc
in ring, ch 12, (sc in ring, ch 8)
twice; repeat from ★ 3 times
more; join with slip st to first
sc, finish off: 4 loops and
8 ch-8 sps.

Note: Loop a short piece of
yarn around any sc to mark
Rnd 1 as **right** side.

Rnd 2: With **right** side facing,
join Color D with dc in any
loop *(see Joining With Dc,
page 27)*; (dc, ch 2, 2 dc) in
same sp, 2 sc in each of next
2 ch-8 sps, ★ (2 dc, ch 2, 2 dc)
in next loop, 2 sc in each of
next 2 ch-8 sps; repeat from ★
2 times **more**; join with slip st
to first dc: 16 dc, 16 sc, and
4 ch-2 sps.

Rnd 3: Ch 3 **(counts as first
dc, now and throughout)**, dc
in next dc, (2 dc, ch 2, 2 dc)
in next corner ch-2 sp, ★ dc in
next 8 sts, (2 dc, ch 2, 2 dc)
in next corner ch-2 sp; repeat
from ★ 2 times **more**, dc in last
6 sts; join with slip st to first
dc, finish off: 48 dc and
4 ch-2 sps.

Rnd 4: With **right** side facing,
join Color A with dc in any
corner ch-2 sp; (dc, ch 2, 2 dc)
in same sp, dc in next 12 dc,
★ (2 dc, ch 2, 2 dc) in next
corner ch-2 sp, dc in next
12 dc; repeat from ★ 2 times
more; join with slip st to first
dc, finish off: 64 dc and
4 ch-2 sps.

Rnd 5: With **right** side facing,
join Color D with dc in any
corner ch-2 sp; (dc, ch 2, 2 dc)
in same sp, dc in next 16 dc,
★ (2 dc, ch 2, 2 dc) in next
corner ch-2 sp, dc in next
16 dc; repeat from ★ 2 times
more; join with slip st to first
dc: 80 dc and 4 ch-2 sps.

Rnd 6: Ch 3, dc in next dc,
(2 dc, ch 2, 2 dc) in next corner
ch-2 sp, ★ dc in next 20 dc,
(2 dc, ch 2, 2 dc) in next corner
ch-2 sp; repeat from ★ 2 times
more, dc in last 18 dc; join
with slip st to first dc, finish off:
96 dc and 4 ch-2 sps.

Rnd 7: With **right** side
facing, join Color A with sc
in any corner ch-2 sp *(see
Joining With Sc, page 27)*; 2 sc
in same sp, (sc in each dc
across to next corner ch-2 sp,
5 sc in ch-2 sp) 3 times, sc in
each dc across, 2 sc in same
sp as first sc; join with slip st
to first sc, finish off leaving a
long end for sewing: 116 sc.

◼◼◻◻ **EASY**

Yarn Requirements for one square:
Color B - 27 yards (24.5 meters)
Color C - 35 yards (32 meters)

Additional Material: Yarn needle

GAUGE: One Motif = 2$\frac{1}{4}$" (5.75 cm) square

MOTIF (Make 4)
With Color B, ch 5; join with slip st to form a ring.

Rnd 1 (Right side)**:** Ch 1, 10 sc in ring; join with slip st to first sc.

Note: Loop a short piece of yarn around any sc to mark Rnd 1 as **right** side.

Rnd 2: Ch 1, sc in same st as joining, 2 sc in next sc, (sc in next sc, 2 sc in next sc) around; join with slip st to first sc: 15 sc.

Rnd 3: Ch 1, sc in same st as joining and in next sc, 2 sc in next sc, (sc in next 2 sc, 2 sc in next sc) around; join with slip st to first sc, finish off: 20 sc.

Rnd 4: With **right** side facing, join Color C with dc in any sc **(see Joining with Dc, page 27)**; dc in same st, sc in next 4 sc, ★ (2 dc, ch 2, 2 dc) in next sc, sc in next 4 sc; repeat from ★ 2 times **more**; 2 dc in same st as first dc, ch 1, sc in first dc to form last corner ch-2 sp: 32 sts and 4 ch-2 sps.

Rnd 5: Ch 1, 3 sc in last ch-2 sp made, sc in next 8 sts, (5 sc in next corner ch-2 sp, sc in next 8 sts) 3 times, 2 sc in same sp as first sc; join with slip st to first sc, finish off leaving a long end for sewing: 52 sc.

Thread yarn needle with long end. With **wrong** sides of 2 Motifs together, beginning in center sc of corner 5-sc group and working through **inside** loops on **both** pieces **(Fig. A)**, whipstitch Motifs together ending in center sc of next corner 5-sc group.

Fig. A

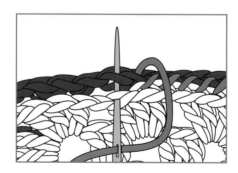

Repeat for remaining 2 Motifs; then whipstitch pieces together to form a Square.

BORDER
Rnd 1: With **right** side facing, join Color C with sc in center sc of any corner 5-sc group **(see Joining With Sc, page 27)**; sc in same st and in next 12 sc, 2 sc in joining, sc in next 12 sc, ★ 3 sc in next corner sc, sc in next 12 sc, 2 sc in joining, sc in next 12 sc; repeat from ★ 2 times **more**, sc in same st as first sc; join with slip st to first sc, finish off: 116 sc.

Rnd 2: With **right** side facing, join Color B with sc in center sc of any corner 3-sc group; sc in same st, ★ sc in next sc and in each sc across to center sc of next corner 3-sc group, 3 sc in center sc; repeat from ★ 2 times **more**, sc in next sc and in each sc across, sc in same st as first sc; join with slip st to first sc: 124 sc.

Rnd 3: Ch 1, 2 sc in same st as joining, ★ sc in next sc and in each sc across to center sc of next corner 3-sc group, 3 sc in center sc; repeat from ★ 2 times **more**, sc in next sc and in each sc across, sc in same st as first sc; join with slip st to first sc, finish off leaving a long end for sewing: 132 sc.

◼️◼️◻️◻️ **EASY +**

Yarn Requirements for one square:
Color D - 10 yards
    (9 meters)
Color E - 35 yards
    (32 meters)

GAUGE: Rnds 1 and 2 = $2^1/_8$"
        (5.4 cm) diameter

With Color E, ch 4; join with slip st to form a ring.

Rnd 1 (Right side)**:** Ch 3 **(counts as first dc, now and throughout)**, 15 dc in ring; join with slip st to first dc, finish off: 16 dc.

Note: Loop a short piece of yarn around any dc to mark Rnd 1 as **right** side.

Rnd 2: With **right** side facing, join Color D with dc in any dc **(see Joining With Dc, page 27)**; dc in same st, 2 dc in next dc and in each dc around; join with slip st to first dc, finish off: 32 dc.

Rnd 3: With **right** side facing, join Color E with dc in any dc; dc in same st and in next dc, (2 dc in next dc, dc in next dc) around; join with slip st to first dc, finish off: 48 dc.

Rnd 4: With **right** side facing, join Color D with dc in any dc; dc in same st and in next 2 dc, (2 dc in next dc, dc in next 2 dc) around; join with slip st to first dc, finish off: 64 dc.

Rnd 5: With **right** side facing, join Color E with sc in any dc **(see Joining With Sc, page 27);** (ch 5, skip next 3 dc, sc in next dc) around to last 3 dc, ch 2, skip last 3 dc, dc in first sc to form last ch-5 sp: 16 sc and 16 ch-5 sps.

Rnd 6: Ch 1, 3 sc in last ch-5 sp made, 5 sc in next ch-5 sp and in each ch-5 sp around, 2 sc in same sp as first sc; join with slip st to first sc: 80 sc.

To work treble crochet (abbreviated tr), YO twice, insert hook in sc indicated, YO and pull up a loop (4 loops on hook), (YO and draw through 2 loops on hook) 3 times.

Rnd 7: Ch 4 **(counts as first tr)**, ★ † tr in next 2 sc, dc in next 2 sc, hdc in next 2 sc, sc in next 7 sc, hdc in next 2 sc, dc in next 2 sc, tr in next 2 sc †, (tr, ch 3, tr) in next sc; repeat from ★ 2 times **more**, then repeat from † to † once, tr in same st as first tr, ch 1, hdc in first tr to form last corner ch-3 sp: 84 sts and 4 ch-3 sps.

Rnd 8: Ch 3, dc in last ch-3 sp made and in next 21 sts, ★ (2 dc, ch 2, 2 dc) in next corner ch-3 sp, dc in next 21 sts; repeat from ★ 2 times **more**, 2 dc in same sp as first dc, ch 1, sc in first dc to form last corner ch-2 sp; finish off leaving a long end for sewing: 100 dc and 4 ch-2 sps.

ribbed

◼◼◻◻ EASY

Yarn Requirements for one square:
Color D - 55 yards (50.5 meters)

GAUGE: In pattern,
14 sts = 3" (7.5 cm);
7 rows = 2" (5 cm)

Ch 29.

Row 1 (Right side)**:** Hdc in third ch from hook **(2 skipped chs count as first hdc)** and in each ch across: 28 hdc.

Note: Loop a short piece of yarn around any hdc to mark Row 1 as **right** side.

To work Back Post double crochet (abbreviated BPdc), YO, insert hook from **back** to **front** around post of st indicated *(Fig. 2, page 28)*, YO and pull up a loop (3 loops on hook), (YO and draw through 2 loops on hook) twice.

Row 2: Ch 2 **(counts as first hdc, now and throughout)**, turn; hdc in next 2 hdc, ★ work BPdc around each of next 2 sts, hdc in next 3 hdc; repeat from ★ across: 18 hdc and 10 BPdc.

To work Front Post double crochet (abbreviated FPdc), YO, insert hook from **front** to **back** around post of st indicated *(Fig. 2, page 28)*, YO and pull up a loop (3 loops on hook), (YO and draw through 2 loops on hook) twice.

Row 3: Ch 2, turn; hdc in next 2 hdc, ★ work FPdc around each of next 2 sts, hdc in next 3 hdc; repeat from ★ across.

Repeat Rows 2 and 3 for pattern until piece measures approximately 6" (15 cm) from beginning ch, ending by working a **right** side row.

Finish off leaving a long end for sewing.

eyelet

◼◼◻◻ EASY

Yarn Requirements for one square:
Color B - 40 yards (36.5 meters)

GAUGE: In pattern,
12 sts = 3" (7.5 cm)

Ch 31.

Row 1 (Right side): Dc in fourth ch from hook **(3 skipped chs count as first dc)** and in each ch across: 29 dc.

Note: Loop a short piece of yarn around any dc to mark Row 1 as **right** side.

Row 2: Ch 4 **(counts as first dc plus ch 1)**, turn; skip next dc, dc in next dc, ★ ch 1, skip next dc, dc in next dc; repeat from ★ across: 15 dc and 14 ch-1 sps.

Row 3: Ch 3 **(counts as first dc)**, turn; dc in next ch-1 sp and in each ch-1 sp and each dc across: 29 dc.

Repeat Rows 2 and 3 for pattern until piece measures approximately 6" (15 cm) from beginning ch, ending by working a **right** side row.

Finish off leaving a long end for sewing.

daisy

EASY +

Yarn Requirements for one square:
Color A - 23 yards
  (21 meters)
Color D - 9 yards (8 meters)
Color E - 18 yards
  (16.5 meters)

GAUGE: Rnds 1-3 = 2¹/₄"
  (5.75 cm) square

With Color D, ch 4; join with slip st to form a ring.

Rnd 1 (Right side)**:** Ch 1, 8 sc in ring; join with slip st to first sc, finish off.

Note: Loop a short piece of yarn around any sc to mark Rnd 1 as **right** side.

To work Puff St (uses one sc), ★ YO, insert hook in sc indicated, YO and pull up a loop; repeat from ★ 3 times **more**, YO and draw through all 9 loops on hook.

Rnd 2: With **right** side facing, join Color A with slip st in any sc; work Puff St in same st, ch 3, (work Puff St in next sc, ch 3) around; join with slip st to first Puff St, finish off: 8 Puff Sts and 8 ch-3 sps.

Rnd 3: With **right** side facing, join Color E with dc in any ch-3 sp *(see Joining With Dc, page 27)*; (dc, ch 3, 2 dc) in same sp, 4 dc in next ch-3 sp, ★ (2 dc, ch 3, 2 dc) in next ch-3 sp, 4 dc in next ch-3 sp; repeat from ★ 2 times **more**; join with slip st to first dc: 32 dc and 4 ch-3 sps.

Rnd 4: Ch 3 **(counts as first dc, now and throughout)**, dc in next dc, (2 dc, ch 3, 2 dc) in next corner ch-3 sp, ★ dc in next 8 dc, (2 dc, ch 3, 2 dc) in next corner ch-3 sp; repeat from ★ 2 times **more**, dc in last 6 dc; join with slip st to first dc: 48 dc and 4 ch-3 sps.

Rnd 5: Ch 3, dc in next 3 dc, (2 dc, ch 3, 2 dc) in next corner ch-3 sp, ★ dc in next 12 dc, (2 dc, ch 3, 2 dc) in next corner ch-3 sp; repeat from ★ 2 times **more**, dc in last 8 dc; join with slip st to first dc, finish off: 64 dc and 4 ch-3 sps.

Rnd 6: With **right** side facing, join Color A with dc in any corner ch-3 sp; (dc, ch 3, 2 dc) in same sp, dc in next 16 dc, ★ (2 dc, ch 3, 2 dc) in next corner ch-3 sp, dc in next 16 dc; repeat from ★ 2 times **more**; join with slip st to first dc: 80 dc and 4 ch-3 sps.

Rnd 7: Ch 3, dc in next dc, (2 dc, ch 3, 2 dc) in next corner ch-3 sp, ★ dc in next 20 dc, (2 dc, ch 3, 2 dc) in next corner ch-3 sp; repeat from ★ 2 times **more**, dc in last 18 dc; join with slip st to first dc, finish off: 96 dc and 4 ch-3 sps.

Rnd 8: With **right** side facing, join Color D with sc in any corner ch-3 sp *(see Joining With Sc, page 27)*; 2 sc in same sp, ★ sc in each dc across to next corner ch-3 sp, 5 sc in corner ch-3 sp; repeat from ★ 2 times **more**, sc in each dc across, 2 sc in same sp as first sc; join with slip st to first sc, finish off leaving a long end for sewing: 116 sc.

diagonal stripes

 INTERMEDIATE

Yarn Requirements for one square:
Color A - 8 yards (7.5 meters)
Color B - 9 yards (8 meters)
Color C - 30 yards
  (27.5 meters)

GAUGE: Row 1 = 1¼"
  (3.25 cm) square

Row 1 (Right side)**:** With Color C, ch 5, 3 dc in fifth ch from hook **(first Block made)**.

Note: Loop a short piece of yarn around any dc to mark Row 1 as **right** side.

To work Beginning Block, ch 5, turn; 3 dc in fourth ch from hook.

To work Block, slip st in ch-3 sp on next Block, ch 3, 3 dc in same sp.

Row 2: Work Beginning Block, slip st in ch-3 sp on first Block, ch 3, 3 dc in same sp, changing to Color B in last dc made *(Fig. 1a, page 27)*: 2 Blocks.

Row 3: Work Beginning Block, slip st in ch-3 sp on first Block, ch 3, 3 dc in same sp, work Block changing to Color C in last dc made: 3 Blocks.

Row 4: Work Beginning Block, slip st in ch-3 sp on first Block, ch 3, 3 dc in same sp, work 2 Blocks: 4 Blocks.

Row 5: Work Beginning Block, slip st in ch-3 sp on first Block, ch 3, 3 dc in same sp, work 3 Blocks changing to Color A in last dc made: 5 Blocks.

Row 6: Work Beginning Block, slip st in ch-3 sp on first Block, ch 3, 3 dc in same sp, work Blocks across changing to Color C in last dc made: 6 Blocks.

Row 7: Work Beginning Block, slip st in ch-3 sp on first Block, ch 3, 3 dc in same sp, work Blocks across: 7 Blocks.

Row 8: Work Beginning Block, slip st in ch-3 sp on first Block, ch 3, 3 dc in same sp, work Blocks across changing to Color B in last dc made: 8 Blocks.

Row 9: Work Beginning Block, slip st in ch-3 sp on first Block, ch 3, 3 dc in same sp, work Blocks across: 9 Blocks.

Row 10: Work Beginning Block, slip st in ch-3 sp on first Block, ch 3, 3 dc in same sp, work Blocks across: 10 Blocks.

Row 11: Ch 1, turn; slip st in first 3 dc and in next ch-3 sp, ch 3, 3 dc in same sp, work Blocks across to last Block, slip st in ch-3 sp on last Block: 9 Blocks.

Row 12: Ch 1, turn; slip st in first 3 dc and in next ch-3 sp changing to Color A in last slip st made, ch 3, 3 dc in same sp, work Blocks across to last Block, slip st in ch-3 sp on last Block: 8 Blocks.

Row 13: Ch 1, turn; slip st in first 3 dc and in next ch-3 sp changing to Color C in last slip st made, ch 3, 3 dc in same sp, work Blocks across to last Block, slip st in ch-3 sp on last Block: 7 Blocks.

Row 14: Repeat Row 11: 6 Blocks.

Row 15: Ch 1, turn; slip st in first 3 dc and in next ch-3 sp changing to Color B in last slip st made, ch 3, 3 dc in same sp, work Block across to last Block, slip st in ch-3 sp on last Block: 5 Blocks.

Rows 16 and 17: Repeat Rows 13 and 14: 3 Blocks.

Row 18: Ch 1, turn; slip st in first 3 dc and in next ch-3 sp changing to Color A in last slip st made, ch 3, 3 dc in same sp, work Block, slip st in ch-3 sp on last Block: 2 Blocks.

Row 19: Ch 1, turn; slip st in first 3 dc and in next ch-3 sp changing to Color C, ch 3, 3 dc in same sp, slip st in ch-3 sp of previous Block; finish off leaving a long end for sewing.

◼◼◻◻ EASY

Yarn Requirements for one square:
Color A - 14 yards (13 meters)
Color B - 14 yards (13 meters)
Color C - 9 yards (8 meters)
Color E - 14 yards (13 meters)

GAUGE: In pattern,
9 sts and 4 rows = 2"
(5 cm)

With Color B, ch 33.

Row 1 (Right side)**:** (Dc, ch 1, dc) in fourth ch from hook **(3 skipped chs count as first dc)**, ★ skip next 2 chs, (dc, ch 1, dc) in next ch; repeat from ★ across to last 2 chs, skip next ch, dc in last ch changing to Color A **(Fig. 1a, page 27)**: 10 ch-1 sps.

Note: Loop a short piece of yarn around any dc to mark Row 1 as **right** side.

Row 2: Ch 3 **(counts as first dc, now and throughout)**, turn; (dc, ch 1, dc) in next ch-1 sp and in each ch-1 sp across, skip next dc, dc in last dc changing to Color E.

Row 3: Ch 3, turn; (dc, ch 1, dc) in next ch-1 sp and in each ch-1 sp across, skip next dc, dc in last dc changing to Color C.

Row 4: Ch 3, turn; (dc, ch 1, dc) in next ch-1 sp and in each ch-1 sp across, skip next dc, dc in last dc changing to Color B.

Row 5: Ch 3, turn; (dc, ch 1, dc) in next ch-1 sp and in each ch-1 sp across, skip next dc, dc in last dc changing to Color A.

Rows 6-15: Repeat Rows 2-5 twice, then repeat Rows 2 and 3 once **more**; at end of Row 15, do **not** change colors; finish off leaving a long end for sewing.

◼◻◻◻ BEGINNER

Yarn Requirements for one square:
Color A - 51 yards
(46.5 meters)

GAUGE: In pattern,
9 sts = 2" (5 cm)

Ch 28.

Row 1 (Wrong side)**:** Dc in third ch from hook **(2 skipped chs count as first hdc)**, sc in next ch, (dc in next ch, sc in next ch) across to last 2 chs, dc in next ch, hdc in last ch: 27 sts.

Note: Loop a short piece of yarn around back of any dc on Row 1 to mark **right** side.

Row 2: Ch 2 **(counts as first hdc, now and throughout)**, turn; sc in next dc, (dc in next sc, sc in next dc) across to last hdc, hdc in last hdc.

Row 3: Ch 2, turn; dc in next sc, (sc in next dc, dc in next sc) across to last hdc, hdc in last hdc.

Repeat Rows 2 and 3 for pattern until piece measures approximately 6" (15 cm) from beginning ch, ending by working a **wrong** side row.

Finish off leaving a long end for sewing.

■■□□ EASY +

Yarn Requirements for one square:

Color B - 24 yards
(22 meters)
Color C - 13 yards
(12 meters)
Color E - 13 yards
(12 meters)

GAUGE: In pattern,
13 sc = 3" (7.5 cm)
6 rows = 1³/₄"
(4.5 cm)

With Color B, ch 27.

Row 1 (Right side)**:** Sc in second ch from hook and in each ch across: 26 sc.

Note: Loop a short piece of yarn around any sc to mark Row 1 as **right** side.

Row 2: Ch 1, turn; sc in each sc across; finish off.

Row 3: With **right** side facing, join Color C with sc in first sc **(see Joining With Sc, page 27)**; sc in next sc and in each sc across.

To work treble crochet (abbreviated tr), YO twice, insert hook in sc indicated, YO and pull up a loop (4 loops on hook), (YO and draw through 2 loops on hook) 3 times.

To work Cross St (uses 3 sc), skip next 2 sc, tr in next sc, ch 1, working in **front** of tr just made **(Fig. 4, page 28)**, tr in first skipped sc.

Row 4: Ch 3 **(counts as first dc, now and throughout)**, turn; work Cross St across to last sc, dc in last sc: 8 Cross Sts.

Row 5: Ch 1, turn; sc in each st and in each ch-1 sp across; finish off: 26 sc.

Row 6: With **right** side facing, join Color B with sc in first sc; sc in next sc and in each sc across.

Rows 7 and 8: Ch 1, turn; sc in each sc across.

Finish off.

Row 9: With **right** side facing, join Color E with sc in first sc; sc in next sc and in each sc across.

Row 10: Ch 3, turn; work Cross St across to last sc, dc in last sc: 8 Cross Sts.

Row 11: Ch 1, turn; sc in each st and in each ch-1 sp across; finish off: 26 sc.

Row 12: With **right** side facing, join Color B with sc in first sc; sc in next sc and in each sc across.

Rows 13 and 14: Ch 1, turn; sc in each sc across.

Finish off.

Row 15: With **right** side facing, join Color C with sc in first sc; sc in next sc and in each sc across.

Row 16: Ch 3, turn; work Cross St across to last sc, dc in last sc: 8 Cross Sts.

Rows 17-23: Repeat Rows 5-11.

Row 24: With **right** side facing, join Color B with sc in first sc; sc in next sc and in each sc across.

Row 25: Ch 1, turn; sc in each sc across; finish off leaving a long end for sewing.

◼◼◻◻ EASY

**Yarn Requirements for
one square:**
Color B - 22 yards
    (20 meters)
Color D - 12 yards
    (11 meters)
Color E - 15 yards
    (13.5 meters)

GAUGE: Rnds 1-3 = 2³/₄"
            (7 cm) square

With Color B, ch 5; join with
slip st to form a ring.

Rnd 1 (Right side)**:** Ch 3
(counts as first dc), 2 dc in
ring, ch 2, (3 dc in ring, ch 2)
3 times; join with slip st to first
dc, finish off: 12 dc and
4 ch-2 sps.

Note: Loop a short piece of
yarn around any dc to mark
Rnd 1 as **right** side.

Rnd 2: With **right** side facing,
join Color E with dc in any
ch-2 sp *(see Joining With Dc,
page 27)*; (dc, ch 2, 2 dc)
in same sp, dc in next 3 dc,
★ (2 dc, ch 2, 2 dc) in next
ch-2 sp, dc in next 3 dc; repeat
from ★ 2 times **more**; join with
slip st to first dc, finish off:
28 dc and 4 ch-2 sps.

Rnd 3: With **right** side facing,
join Color D with dc in any
corner ch-2 sp; (dc, ch 2, 2 dc)
in same sp, dc in next 7 dc,
★ (2 dc, ch 2, 2 dc) in next
corner ch-2 sp, dc in next
7 dc; repeat from ★ 2 times
more; join with slip st to
first dc, finish off: 44 dc and
4 ch-2 sps.

Rnd 4: With **right** side facing,
join Color B with dc in any
corner ch-2 sp; (dc, ch 2,
2 dc) in same sp, dc in next
11 dc, ★ (2 dc, ch 2, 2 dc)
in next corner ch-2 sp, dc in
next 11 dc; repeat from ★
2 times **more**; join with slip st
to first dc, finish off: 60 dc and
4 ch-2 sps.

Rnd 5: With **right** side facing,
join Color E with dc in any
corner ch-2 sp; (dc, ch 2,
2 dc) in same sp, dc in next
15 dc, ★ (2 dc, ch 2, 2 dc)
in next corner ch-2 sp, dc in
next 15 dc; repeat from ★
2 times **more**; join with slip st
to first dc, finish off: 76 dc and
4 ch-2 sps.

Rnd 6: With **right** side facing,
join Color D with dc in any
corner ch-2 sp; (dc, ch 2, 2 dc)
in same sp, dc in next 19 dc,
★ (2 dc, ch 2, 2 dc) in next
corner ch-2 sp, dc in next
19 dc; repeat from ★ 2 times
more; join with slip st to
first dc, finish off: 92 dc and
4 ch-2 sps.

Rnd 7: With **right** side facing,
join Color B with dc in any
corner ch-2 sp; ch 2, 2 dc in
same sp, dc in next 23 dc,
★ (2 dc, ch 2, 2 dc) in next
corner ch-2 sp, dc in next
23 dc; repeat from ★ 2 times
more, dc in same sp as first
dc; join with slip st to first dc,
finish off leaving a long end for
sewing: 108 dc and 4 ch-2 sps.

star

◼◼◻◻ EASY

Yarn Requirements for one square:
Color A - 32 yards
(29.5 meters)
Color C - 12 yards
(11 meters)
Color D - 7 yards
(6.5 meters)

GAUGE: Rnds 1-3 = 2³/₄"
(7 cm) diameter

With Color D, ch 4; join with slip st to form a ring.

Rnd 1 (Right side)**:** Ch 1, ★ sc in ring, [ch 5, sc in second ch from hook and in next 3 chs **(spoke made)]**; repeat from ★ 4 times **more**; join with slip st to first sc, finish off: 5 sc and 5 spokes.

Note: Loop a short piece of yarn around any sc to mark Rnd 1 as **right** side.

To work treble crochet
(abbreviated tr), YO twice, insert hook in sc indicated, YO and pull up a loop (4 loops on hook), (YO and draw through 2 loops on hook) 3 times.

To work double treble crochet
(abbreviated dtr), YO 3 times, insert hook in sc indicated, YO and pull up a loop (5 loops on hook), (YO and draw through 2 loops on hook) 4 times.

Rnd 2: With **right** side facing, join Color A with sc in skipped ch at tip of any spoke **(see Joining With Sc, page 27)**; skip next 4 sc on same spoke, (dtr, 2 tr, dtr) in next sc (between spokes), ★ sc in skipped ch at tip of next spoke, skip next 4 sc on same spoke, (dtr, 2 tr, dtr) in next sc (between spokes); repeat from ★ 3 times **more**; join with slip st to first sc: 25 sts.

Rnd 3: Ch 1, sc in same st and in next dtr, 2 hdc in each of next 2 tr, (sc in next 3 sts, 2 hdc in each of next 2 tr) 4 times, 2 sc in last dtr; join with slip st to first sc, finish off: 36 sts.

Rnd 4: With **right** side facing, join Color C with dc in same st as joining **(see Joining With Dc, page 27)**; (dc, ch 2, 2 dc) in same st, dc in next sc, hdc in next 2 hdc, sc in next 2 hdc, hdc in next 2 sc, dc in next sc, ★ (2 dc, ch 2, 2 dc) in next st, dc in next st, hdc in next 2 sts, sc in next 2 sts, hdc in next 2 sts, dc in next st; repeat from ★ 2 times **more**; join with slip st to first dc, finish off: 48 sts and 4 ch-2 sps.

Rnd 5: With **right** side facing, join Color D with sc in any corner ch-2 sp; 2 sc in same sp, sc in next 12 sts, (3 sc in next corner ch-2 sp, sc in next 12 sts) around; join with slip st to first sc, finish off: 60 sc.

Rnd 6: With **right** side facing, join Color A with dc in center sc of any corner 3-sc group; dc in next 14 sc, ★ (dc, ch 2, dc) in next corner sc, dc in next 14 sc; repeat from ★ 2 times **more**, dc in same st as first dc, ch 1, sc in first dc to form last corner ch-2 sp: 64 dc and 4 ch-2 sps.

Rnd 7: Ch 3 **(counts as first dc, now and throughout)**, dc in last ch-2 sp made, ★ dc in next 16 dc, (2 dc, ch 2, 2 dc) in next corner ch-2 sp; repeat from ★ 2 times **more**, dc in last 16 dc, 2 dc in same sp as first dc, ch 1, sc in first dc to form last corner ch-2 sp: 80 dc and 4 ch-2 sps.

Rnd 8: Ch 3, dc in last ch-2 sp made, ★ dc in next 20 dc, (2 dc, ch 2, 2 dc) in next corner ch-2 sp; repeat from ★ 2 times **more**, dc in last 20 dc, 2 dc in same sp as first dc, ch 2; join with slip st to first dc, finish off: 96 dc and 4 ch-2 sps.

Rnd 9: With **right** side facing, join Color C with sc in any corner ch-2 sp; sc in same sp and in next 24 dc, (3 sc in next corner ch-2 sp, sc in next 24 dc) 3 times, sc in same sp as first sc; join with slip st to first sc, finish off leaving a long end for sewing: 108 sc.

teardrops

■■□□ EASY +

Yarn Requirements for one square:
Color A - 21 yards (19 meters)
Color B - 21 yards (19 meters)
Color C - 27 yards
   (24.5 meters)

GAUGE: In pattern,
   12 sts = 2$\frac{1}{2}$"
   (6.25 cm);
   6 rows = 2" (5 cm)

With Color C, ch 30.

Row 1 (Right side)**:** Sc in second ch from hook and in next ch, ch 1, (skip next ch, sc in next 3 chs, ch 1) across to last 3 chs, skip next ch, sc in last 2 chs: 22 sc and 7 ch-1 sps.

Note: Loop a short piece of yarn around any sc to mark Row 1 as **right** side.

Row 2: Ch 3 **(counts as first dc, now and throughout)**, turn; dc in next sc, ch 1, (skip next ch-1 sp, dc in next 3 sc, ch 1) across to last ch-1 sp, skip last ch-1 sp, dc in last 2 sc; finish off.

To work treble crochet (abbreviated tr), YO twice, insert hook in skipped st indicated, YO and pull up a loop (4 loops on hook), (YO and draw through 2 loops on hook) 3 times.

Work in the following color sequence: ★ 2 Rows **each** of Color A, Color B, Color C; repeat from ★ for color sequence.

Row 3: With **right** side facing, join next color with sc in first dc **(see Joining With Sc, page 27)**; sc in next dc, working **around** previous 2 rows **(Fig. 3, page 28)**, tr in first skipped ch on beginning ch, ★ sc in next dc, ch 1, skip next dc, sc in next dc, working **around** previous 2 rows, tr in next skipped ch on beginning ch; repeat from ★ across to last 2 dc, sc in last 2 dc: 23 sts and 6 ch-1 sps.

Row 4: Ch 3, turn; dc in next 3 sts, ch 1, (skip next ch-1 sp, dc in next 3 sts, ch 1) across to last ch-1 sp, skip last ch-1 sp, dc in last 4 sts; finish off.

Row 5: With **right** side facing, join next color with sc in first dc; sc in next dc, ch 1, ★ skip next dc, sc in next dc, working **around** previous 2 rows, tr in next skipped dc 3 rows **below**, sc in next dc, ch 1; repeat from ★ across to last 3 dc, skip next dc, sc in last 2 dc: 22 sts and 7 ch-1 sps.

Row 6: Ch 3, turn; dc in next sc, ch 1, (skip next ch-1 sp, dc in next 3 sts, ch 1) across to last ch-1 sp, skip last ch-1 sp, dc in last 2 sc; finish off.

Row 7: With **right** side facing, join next color with sc in first dc; sc in next dc, working **around** previous 2 rows, tr in next skipped dc 3 rows **below**, ★ sc in next dc, ch 1, skip next dc, sc in next dc, working **around** previous 2 rows, tr in next skipped dc 3 rows **below**; repeat from ★ across to last 2 dc, sc in last 2 dc: 23 sts and 6 ch-1 sps.

Rows 8-24: Repeat Rows 4-7, 4 times; then repeat Row 4 once **more**.

Row 25: With **right** side facing, join Color C with sc in first dc; ★ sc in next 3 dc, working **around** previous 2 rows, tr in next skipped dc 3 rows **below**; repeat from ★ across to last 4 dc, sc in last 4 dc: 29 sts.

Row 26: Ch 3, turn; dc in next sc and in each st across; finish off leaving a long end for sewing.

ABBREVIATIONS

BPdc   Back Post double crochet
ch(s)   chain(s)
cm   centimeters
dc   double crochet(s)
dtr   double treble crochet
FPdc   Front Post double crochet
hdc   half double crochet(s)
mm   millimeters
Rnd(s) Round(s)
sc   single crochet(s)
sp(s)   space(s)
st(s)   stitch(es)
tr   treble crochet(s)
YO   yarn over

★ — work instructions following ★ as many **more** times as indicated in addition to the first time.

† to † — work all instructions from first † to second † **as many** times as specified.

( ) or **[ ]** — work enclosed instructions **as many** times as specified by the number immediately following **or** work all enclosed instructions in the stitch or space indicated **or** contains explanatory remarks.

colon (:) — the number given after a colon at the end of a row or round denotes the number of stitches or spaces you should have on that row or round.

CROCHET TERMINOLOGY	
UNITED STATES	INTERNATIONAL
slip stitch (slip st) =	single crochet (sc)
single crochet (sc) =	double crochet (dc)
half double crochet (hdc) =	half treble crochet (htr)
double crochet (dc) =	treble crochet(tr)
treble crochet (tr) =	double treble crochet (dtr)
double treble crochet (dtr) =	triple treble crochet (ttr)
triple treble crochet (tr tr) =	quadruple treble crochet (qtr)
skip =	miss

CROCHET HOOKS													
U.S.	B-1	C-2	D-3	E-4	F-5	G-6	H-8	I-9	J-10	K-10$\frac{1}{2}$	N	P	Q
Metric - mm	2.25	2.75	3.25	3.5	3.75	4	5	5.5	6	6.5	9	10	15

■□□□ BEGINNER	Projects for first-time crocheters using basic stitches. Minimal shaping.
■■□□ EASY	Projects using yarn with basic stitches, repetitive stitch patterns, simple color changes, and simple shaping and finishing.
■■■□ INTERMEDIATE	Projects using a variety of techniques, such as basic lace patterns or color patterns, mid-level shaping and finishing.
■■■■ EXPERIENCED	Projects with intricate stitch patterns, techniques and dimension, such as non-repeating patterns, multi-color techniques, fine threads, small hooks, detailed shaping and refined finishing.

Yarn Weight Symbol & Names	LACE ⓪	SUPER FINE ①	FINE ②	LIGHT ③	MEDIUM ④	BULKY ⑤	SUPER BULKY ⑥
Type of Yarns in Category	Fingering, 10-count crochet thread	Sock, Fingering Baby	Sport, Baby	DK, Light Worsted	Worsted, Afghan, Aran	Chunky, Craft, Rug	Bulky, Roving
Crochet Gauge* Ranges in Single Crochet to 4" (10 cm)	32-42 double crochets**	21-32 sts	16-20 sts	12-17 sts	11-14 sts	8-11 sts	5-9 sts
Advised Hook Size Range	Steel*** 6,7,8 Regular hook B-1	B-1 to E-4	E-4 to 7	7 to I-9	I-9 to K-10.5	K-10.5 to M-13	M-13 and larger

*GUIDELINES ONLY: The chart above reflects the most commonly used gauges and hook sizes for specific yarn categories.

** Lace weight yarns are usually crocheted on larger-size hooks to create lacy openwork patterns. Accordingly, a gauge range is difficult to determine. Always follow the gauge stated in your pattern.

*** Steel crochet hooks are sized differently from regular hooks–the higher the number the smaller the hook, which is the reverse of regular hook sizing.

GAUGE

Exact gauge is **essential** for proper size. Before beginning your project, make a sample swatch in the yarn and hook specified in the individual instructions. After completing the swatch, measure it, counting your stitches and rows or rounds carefully. If your swatch is larger or smaller than specified, **make another, changing hook size to get the correct gauge**. Keep trying until you find the size hook that will give you the specified gauge.

JOINING WITH SC

When instructed to join with sc, begin with a slip knot on hook. Insert hook in stitch or space indicated, YO and pull up a loop, YO and draw through both loops on hook.

JOINING WITH DC

When instructed to join with dc, begin with a slip knot on hook. YO, holding loop on hook, insert hook in stitch or space indicated, YO and pull up a loop (3 loops on hook), (YO and draw through 2 loops on hook) twice.

CHANGING COLORS

Work the last stitch to within one step of completion (2 loops on hook), drop yarn to **wrong** side, hook new yarn **(Figs. 1a & b)** and draw through both loops on hook. When using two colors across one row, carry unused color loosely across **wrong** side of work. When working **next** row, work over carried strand **(Fig. 1c)**. Cut yarn when no longer needed.

Fig. 1a

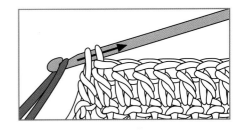

Fig. 1b

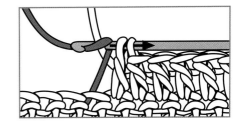

Fig. 1c

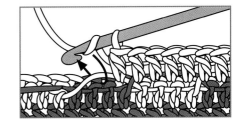

POST STITCH

Work around post of stitch indicated, inserting hook in direction of arrow *(Fig. 2)*.

Fig. 2

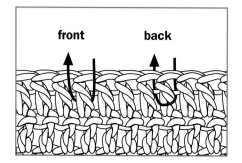

WORKING AROUND A STITCH

Work in stitch or space indicated, inserting hook in direction of arrow *(Fig. 3)*.

Fig. 3

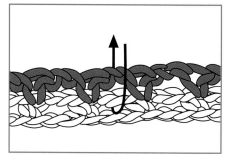

WORKING IN FRONT OF A STITCH

Work in stitch or space indicated, inserting hook in direction of arrow *(Fig. 4)*.

Fig. 4

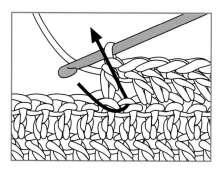

BLOCKING

Follow the instructions on the yarn label or block as follows: For wool, steam the Square supporting the weight of the iron at all times. Allow the Square to dry flat, away from heat or sunlight.

For synthetic and blends, submerge the Square in cool water. Roll the Square in a clean terry towel and gently press out the excess moisture. Lay the Square flat and allow to dry completely, away from heat and sunlight.

WHIPSTITCH

Place two Squares with **wrong** sides together. Beginning in center of corner, sew through both pieces once to secure the beginning of the seam, leaving an ample yarn end to weave in later. Insert the needle from **back** to **front** through both loops *(Fig. 5a)* **or** in end of rows *(Fig. 5b)* on both Squares. Bring the needle around and insert it from **back** to **front** through next loops on both Squares. Continue in this manner across to corner, keeping the sewing yarn fairly loose.

Fig. 5a

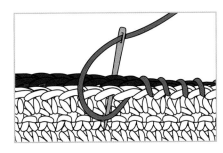

Fig. 5b

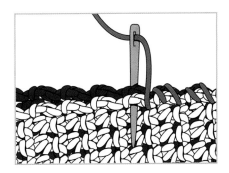

The squares and wraps in this leaflet were made using light weight yarn. Any brand of light weight yarn may be used. It is best to refer to the yardage/meters when determining how many balls or skeins to purchase. Remember, to arrive at the finished size, it is the GAUGE/TENSION that is important, not the brand of yarn.

For your convenience, listed below are the specific yarns used to create our photography models.

ALTERNATING RIB WRAP
Bernat® Softee® Baby
Color D - #30185 Soft Lilac

BABY SAMPLER
Lion Brand® Babysoft®
Color A - #191 Violet
Color B - #157 Pastel Yellow
Color C - #143 Lavender
Color D - #100 White
Color E - #156 Pastel Green

CONCENTRIC CIRCLES WRAP
Red Heart® Soft Baby®
Color D - #7001 White
Color E - #7624 Lime
#7588 Lilac
#7737 Powder Pink
#7321 Powder Yellow
#7680 New Mint
#7881 Powder Blue

FOUR SQUARE WRAP
Red Heart® Designer Sport™
Color A - #3801 Aqua Ice
Color D - #3101 Ivory
Color E - #3620 Celadon

STAR & EYELET WRAP
Bernat® Softee® Baby
Color A - #02002 Pale Blue
Colors B & D - #02003 Lemon
Color C - #02004 Mint

STITCH GALLERY
Lion Brand® Babysoft®
Color A - #191 Violet
Color B - #157 Pastel Yellow
Color C - #143 Lavender
Color D - #100 White
Color E - #156 Pastel Green

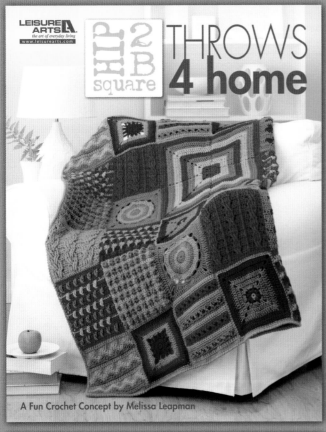

HIP 2 B square

Discover more of Melissa Leapman's innovative patterns!

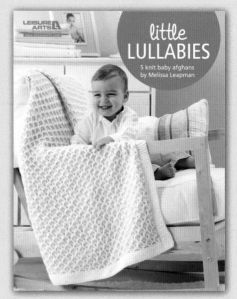

#4528 Little Lullabies   #5153 Cardigans with a Conscience   #3845 Dynamic Designs

These knitting and crochet publications by this talented designer are filled with fresh projects.
For birthdays, baby showers, housewarming, or just because—the perfect gift ideas are right here!

Find these Melissa Leapman pattern books and more at
your local craft retailer or at www.LeisureArts.com.

We have made every effort to ensure that these instructions are accurate and complete. We cannot, however, be responsible for human error, typographical mistakes, or variations in individual work.

Production Team: Writer/Technical Editor - Lindsay Diane White; Contributing Editors - Linda Daley, Sarah Green, and Cathy Hardy; Editorial Writer - Susan McManus Johnson; Senior Graphic Artist - Dana Vaughn; Graphic Artist - Janie Wright; Photography Manager - Katherine Laughlin; Photo Stylist - Sandra Daniel; and Photographer - Ken West.

Squares and Wraps made and instructions tested by Janet Akins, Marianna Crowder, Raymelle Greening, Trudy Kumpe, Katherine May, Margaret Taverner, and Annie Mary Wilson.

For digital downloads of Leisure Arts' best-selling designs, visit http://www.leisurearts.com